Guided reading notes

by Kate Ruttle (series editor)

Trackers level 2: Frog tracks

Sand, Kippers or Aliens

Genre: non-fiction	**Text type:** instruction/ procedural	**Author:** Sarah Fleming

Do you get bored with board games for indoor playtime? Here are three ideas for games you can play in the classroom.

High frequency words	Phonics		Content words and Tricky words
a, and, are, but, can, do, first, for, go, have, here, how, in, is, it, like, look, make, me, next, of, on, one, put, that, the, these, they, this, three, to, two, up, use, we, what's, when, with, you, your	**Words with consonant blends** *blow, draw, end, fewest, floor, fold, kind, number, place, player, point, sand, spade, start, steady, stop, swim, throw, tray, try, want*	**Useful long vowel phonemes** 'ue' in *fewest, move, oops, room, scoop, to, too, two, tube(s), use, who, you* 'ee' in *being, me, need, people, sleeps, these, three, we*	*alien, bored, coin, fewest, finally, finish, fold, half, newspaper, point, pudding, ready steady, scissors, why, whole*

Guided reading

The aim of this series is to encourage children to read for meaning. This booklet provides page-by-page notes suggesting a variety of ways to do this.

Guided reading could be covered in three stages:

1 Introduce the book
2 Read the book
3 Revisit the book

For guidance on how to go through these stages, see the back cover.

Main text is always on a yellow background. This is the text that the children should try to read independently. It contains a high proportion of high frequency and phonically regular words.

Other texts present a higher level of challenge, but most children should be able to read it with some support.

Independent reading

This book can be used for independent reading. To help children read for meaning, use some of the ideas from the 'Read the book' notes on the back cover.

Asking questions

Encourage the children to ask questions of you and of each other as both asking and answering questions develops comprehension. Throughout their reading, use the italicised questions to make children think about the meaning of both individual words and bigger text.

Phonics and high frequency words

In the 'Follow on' boxes there is information about phonically regular words on the pages. If children get stuck on these words, they can be encouraged to 'sound them out'. The high frequency words listed are all from the *Trackers* Frog Tracks High Frequency Word list (see Teacher's Guide) and are words that children need to learn to recognise.

For notes on phonics and high frequency words plus general information on how to teach these in the *Trackers* Teacher's Guide for levels 1 and 2.

Pages 2 and 3

1 Heading

★ If your school uses a different term to describe indoor playtime, tell the children your equivalent of this term.
★ *Why do you think it is called 'wet play?'*
★ *What do you do during wet play?*

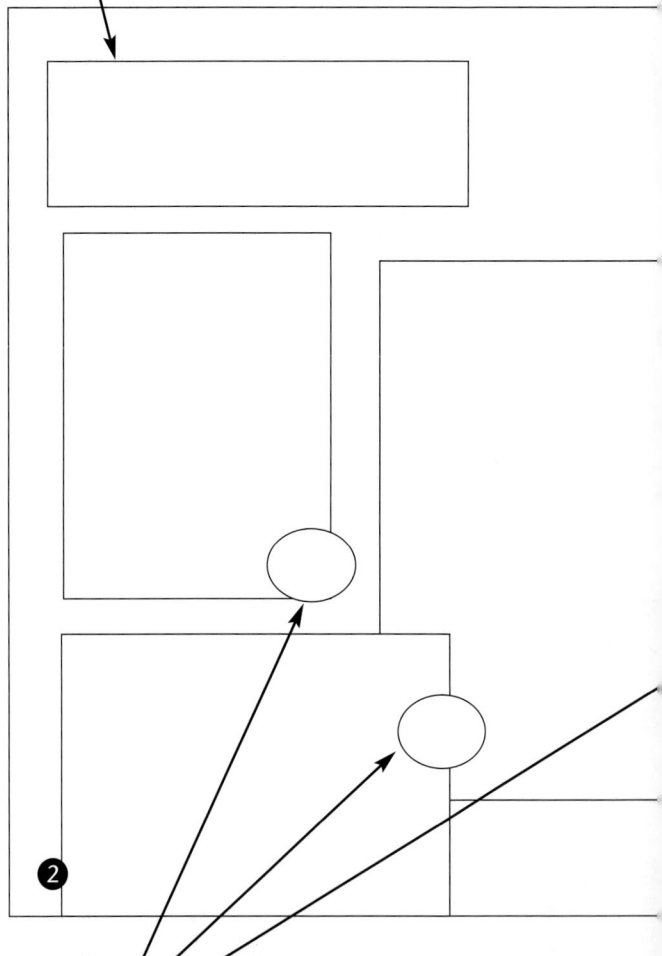

❷

3 Pictures and secondary text

★ *What are the children doing in each of these pictures?*
Is this the kind of thing you do during wet play?
★ *Talk about the use of question marks at the end of each caption.*
Why are they there?

Tricky words

★ There are no unfamiliar main text words.

Words and sentences

★ Talk about the different punctuation on the page and make sure the children know what the function of each is.

★ Look at the word *board*. Can the children segment it into three phonemes: *b-oar-d*? Now write the word *bored* and identify the phonemes again: *b-or-ed*. Talk about the difference in meaning between the two words and how you can recognise which one is a verb past tense (*ed* ending).

Making meaning

★ Ask the children what expectations does this introduction raise for the rest of the book?

★ Talk about the background image.

★ *Why do you think there are some photographs and some illustrations on the page?*

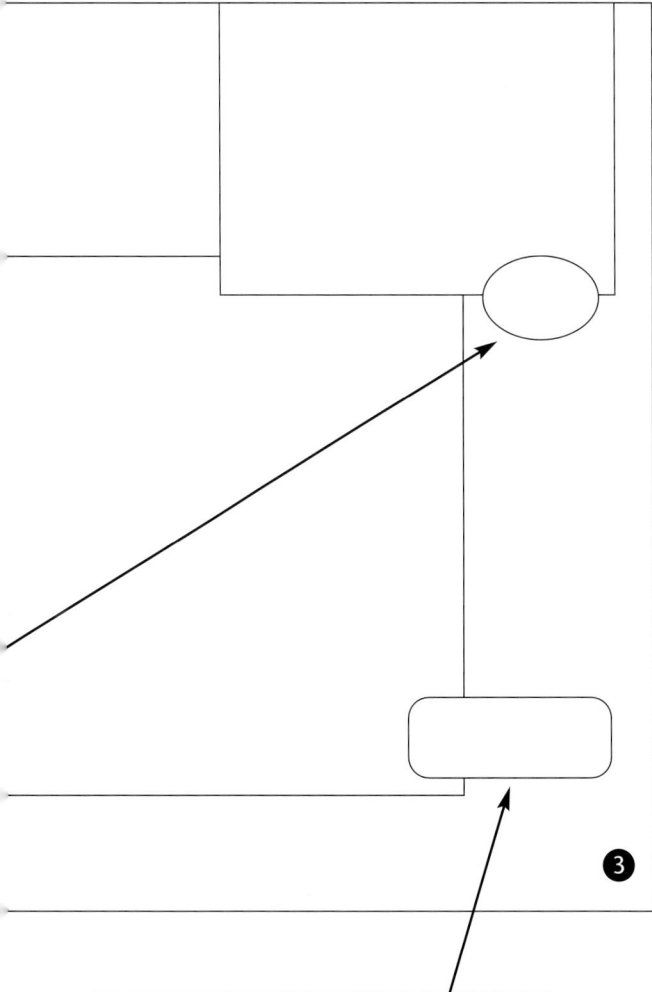

3

2 Main text

★ This text introduces what follows in the book.

★ Point out to the children that these pages are the introduction to the topic in the book.

Pages 4 and 5

4 Heading
★ **vocabulary check:** *pudding*
★ *Why do you think the game is called Sand Pudding?*
What is a pudding more usually made of?

5 Main text
★ **vocabulary check:** *coin*
★ Talk about all the information in this panel.
Which words are usually found at the beginning of an instruction text?
(answer: both the goal/aim and the 'You will need' list)

6 Main text
★ **vocabulary check:** *finally*
★ Read the sequence of instructions.
What do these instructions tell you about? (answer: preparing to play the game, not playing the game)

❹

7 Subheading and main text

★ vocabulary check: *point, fewest*
★ *What do this set of instructions tell you how to do?*
★ *How do you win the game?*

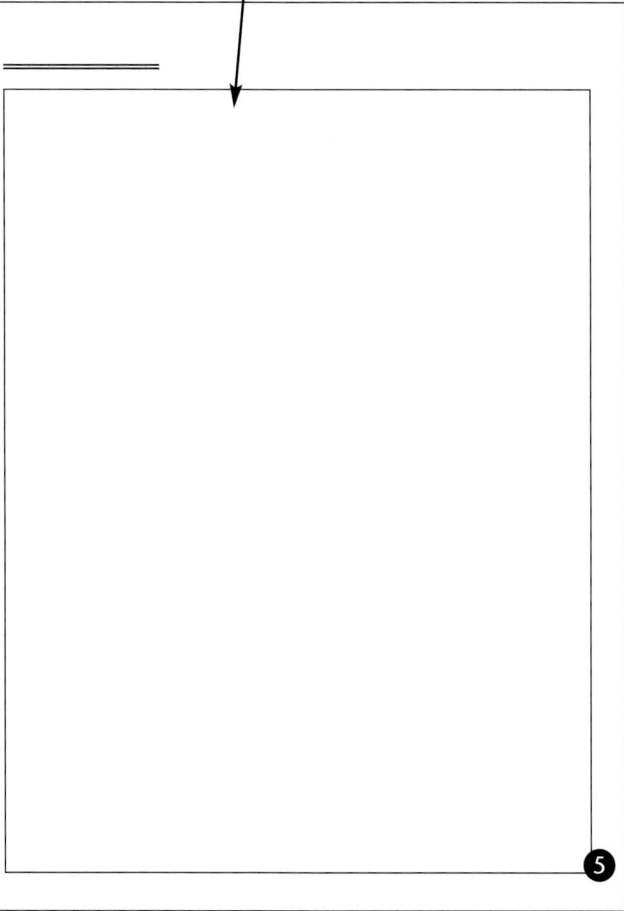

⑤

Tricky words

★ *fewest* (Ask the children to split the word into syllables: *few-est*. The first syllable has the tricky bit *ew*. Link to dew, grew, new. The children should recognise the suffix *est* for the second syllable in context of few, fewer, fewest.)
★ *pudding* (The tricky bit is the short vowel sound in the first syllable. Link with put rather than cut and hut. Remind children of the need for the double consonant before the *ing* following a short vowel sound.)
★ *coin* and *point* (These words have a regular *oi* letter pattern for this long vowel phoneme when it is not at the end of a word or syllable.)
★ *finally* (The tricky bit is the *lly*. Cover up the *ly* so that the children can read 'final'. Do they recognise the *ly* as the common adverb-forming suffix?)

Words and sentences

★ Look at the first word in each box on page 4. *Why are these words used in instructions?*

Making meaning

★ Talk about how the sequence of boxes is marked differently on each of the pages. Ask the children which they find clearer and ask them why.
★ Talk about the background. *Why has it been chosen?*

Pages 6 and 7

8 Heading
★ Do the children know what a kipper is?
(answer: a smoked herring)

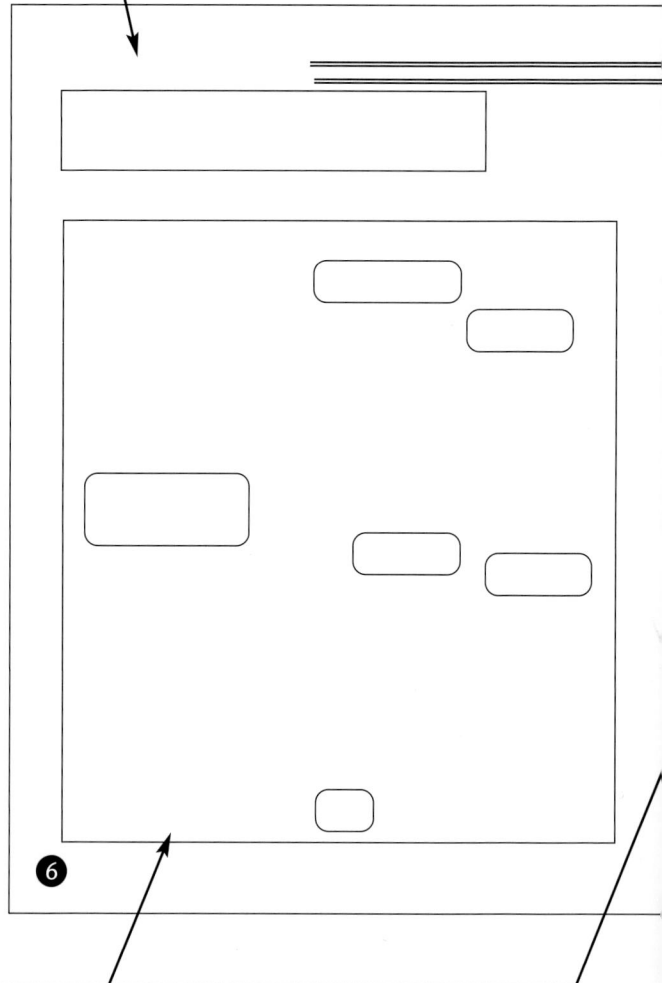

9 Main text
★ Talk about the presentation of this set of instructions.
Is it conventional (do all instructions always look like this)? Why not?
When do children normally expect to see this kind of presentation?
★ All of the text is main text. The bordering colour only indicates who is speaking each time. (The children could read this text as a play, with each child reading one coloured speech bubble – there are five characters.)

6

Tricky words

★ *scissors* (There are two tricky bits here. The silent c in the –sc– letter pattern, make links to scene. The second tricky bit is the pronunciation of the –ss– letter pattern.)

Words and sentences

★ Can the children identify the speech bubbles which are not sentences? (answer: *me too; Me! Me!; And me!; Me*)

Making meaning

★ *Have any instructions been given on these pages?* (answer: *wait* and *see*) Remind children to look for a verb at the beginning of a sentence in an instruction.

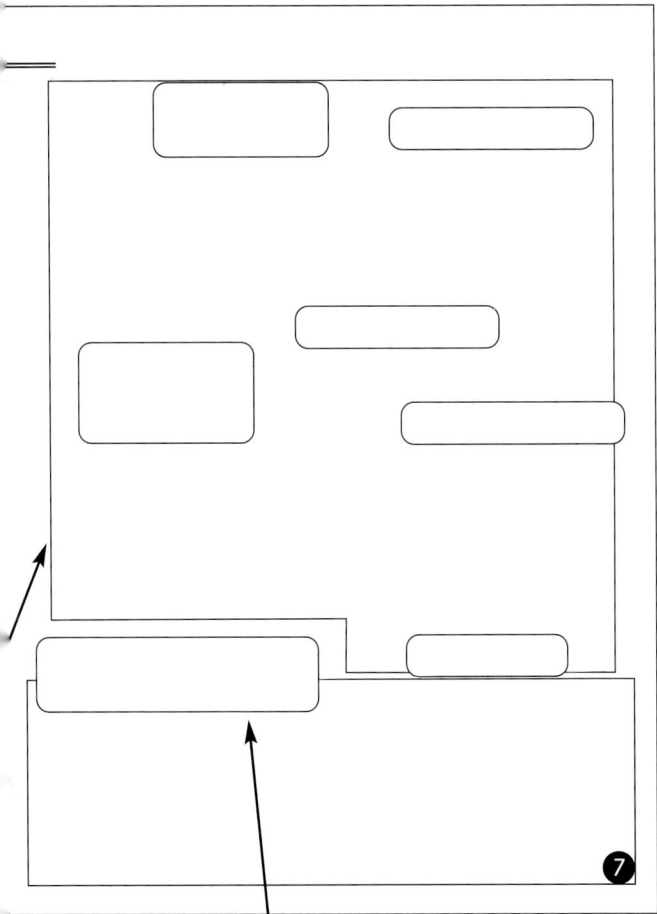

10 Main text

★ **vocabulary check:** *scissors*
★ Do children recognise the function of this speech bubble? (answer: it is the familiar 'You will need' at the beginning of a set of instructions)

Pages 8 and 9

11 Subheading
★ This type of subheading is used throughout the book to show that a game is continuing.

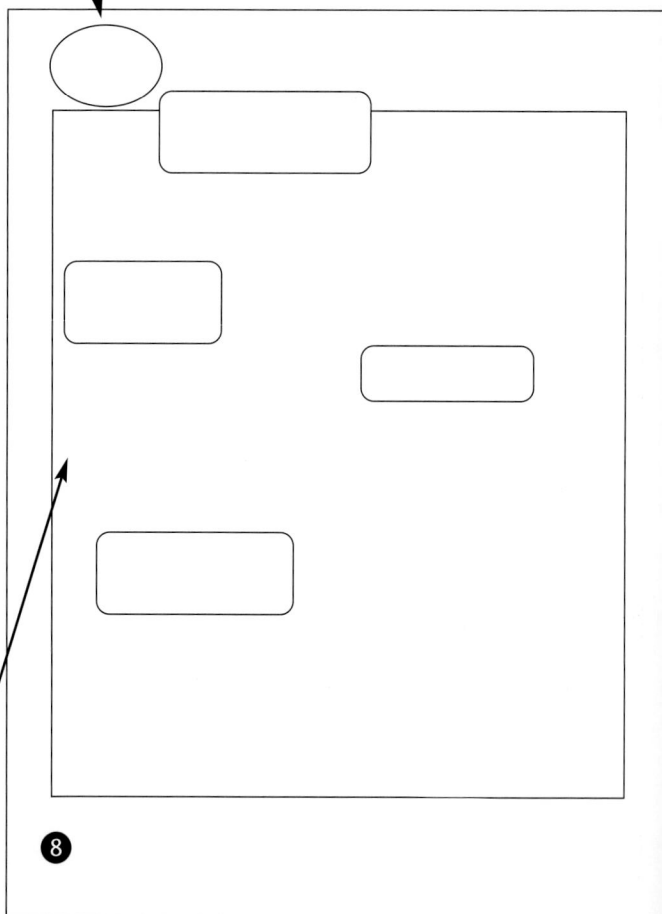

8

12 Main text
★ **vocabulary check:** *fold, half*
★ This is where the more conventional instructional language begins. Point out how the illustrations closely match the instructions.

Tricky words

★ *fold* (Use onset and rhyme to link with old, g-old, t-old, b-old, c-old.)
★ *half* (The tricky bit is the <u>al</u>, make links to calf, calm, palm.)

Words and sentences

★ Can the children find verbs at the beginning of sentences which mark typical instructions? (answer: *Look, Fold, Draw, Cut*)

Making meaning

★ Talk about the different kinds of language on the page, e.g. instructions on the left, more informal chat on the right.
How are they different?
★ Focus on features such as, verbs at the beginning of sentences in the instructions versus non-sentences, questions and comments on the right.

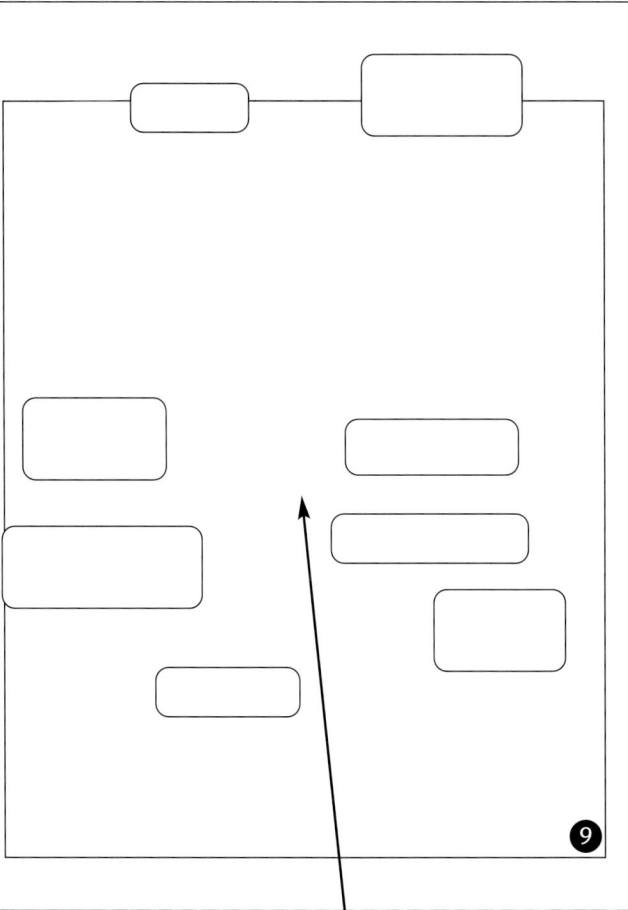

9

13 Main text

★ *Are the instructions continuing here? How do you know?*
★ *Only one of the speech bubbles around the table is an instruction. Which one? (Look at my kipper!)*

Pages 10 and 11

14 Subheading

★ *Is this a new game?*
  How do you know?

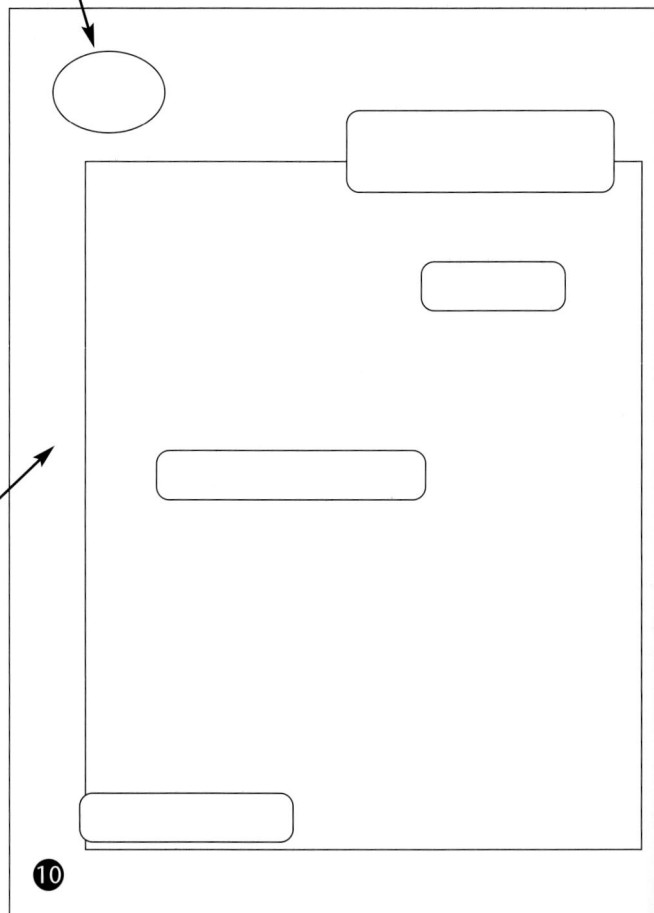

15 Main text

★ *What kind of language
  is this?
  Can you find two speech
  bubbles on the page
  containing instructions?
  (answer: both the
  teacher's speech bubbles)*

🔟

16 Main text

★ **vocabulary check:** *ready steady, newspaper, why*

★ *Look at the language on this page. Which bits are instructions? How do you recognise them?*

⓫

Tricky words

★ *why* (Ask the children to segment the word into phonemes: *wh-y*. Both are familiar. Link *wh* to when, what, where etc. and the *y* to sky, fly, my etc.)

★ *ready steady* (This is predictable from the context. Can children find the rhyming strings *(eady)*? The tricky bit in these words is the *ea* making the short vowel phoneme 'e'. This is not unusual before *d*.)

★ *newspaper* (Break this compound word into two: *news-paper.*)

Words and sentences

★ *How many different punctuation marks can you find?*
Can the children tell you what each one indicates?

Making meaning

★ *Can the children explain to you what the function of the newspaper is? Do the kippers really swim?*

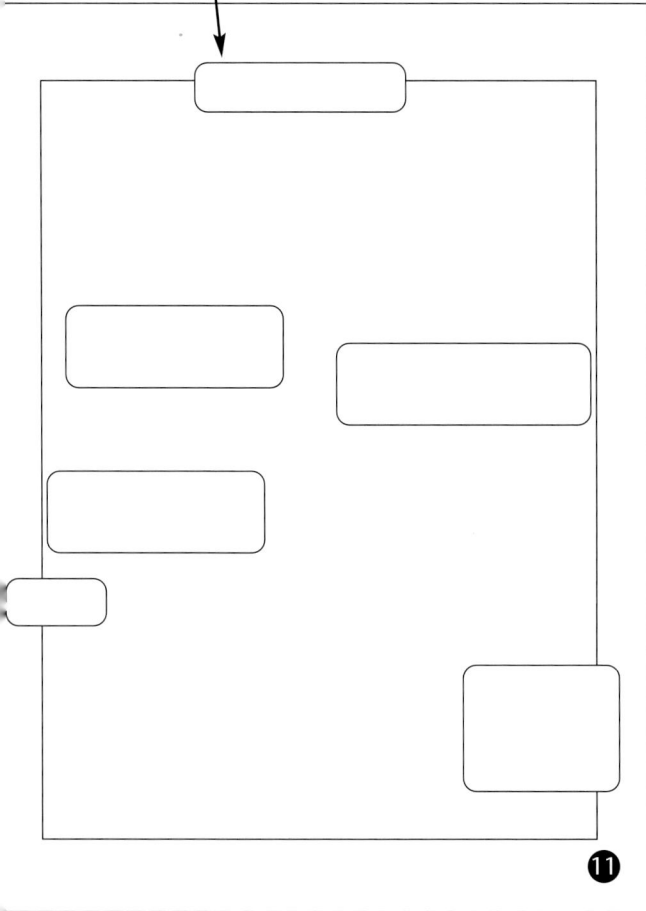

Pages 12 and 13

17 Subheading
★ *Is this a new game?*
How do you know?

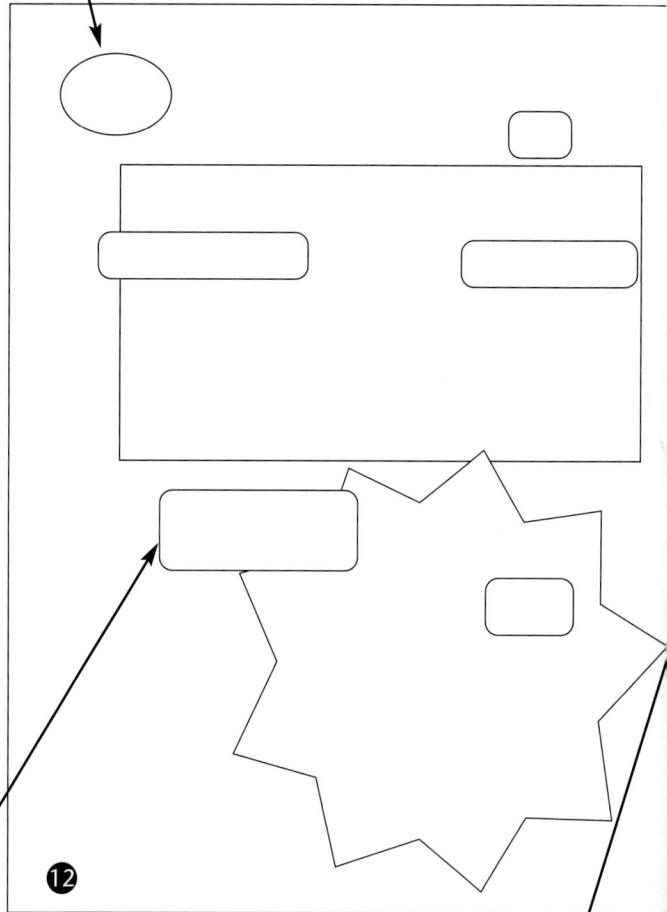

18 Main text
★ *Are there any instructions on this page?*
What kind of language is it?

20 Main text
★ Can the children identify features of
a conventional instruction text here?
(answer: *aim* and *you will need*)

19 Heading

★ **vocabulary check:** *alien, whole*
★ *Is this a new game? How do you know?*

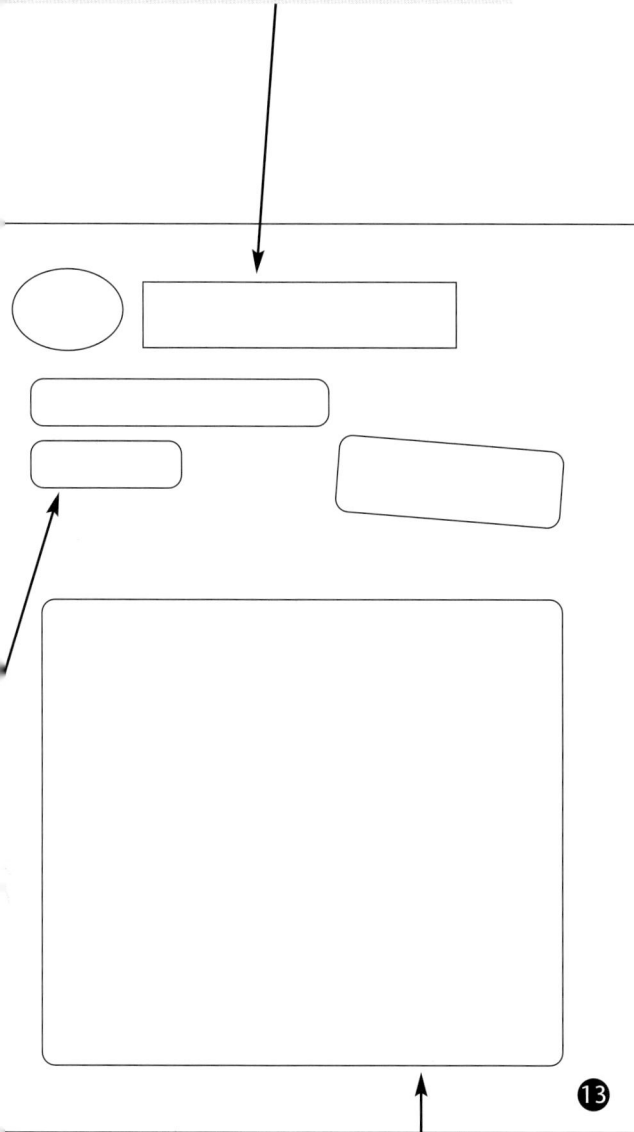

Tricky words

★ *alien* (In this word, each letter represents a phoneme: *a-l-i-e-n.*)
★ *whole* (The tricky bit is the <u>wh</u> letter string, make links to when, where, what etc.)

Words and sentences

★ Talk about the words *winning* and *winner*. *Why do they both have double n, when win only has one?*
Remind the children about the need to double consonants after short vowels before *ing.*

Making meaning

★ *How do you win the Kipper Race game? How do you know?*
★ Ask the children to look back through the pages. Was the winner always keen to play the game?

⑬

21 Subheading and main text

★ *Which bit is the subheading? How do you know?*
★ Make sure the children understand how the game works. If they are familiar with Beetle Drives, they should recognise the similarities.

13

Pages 14, 15 and 16

22 Subheading

★ *Is this a new game? Why not?*

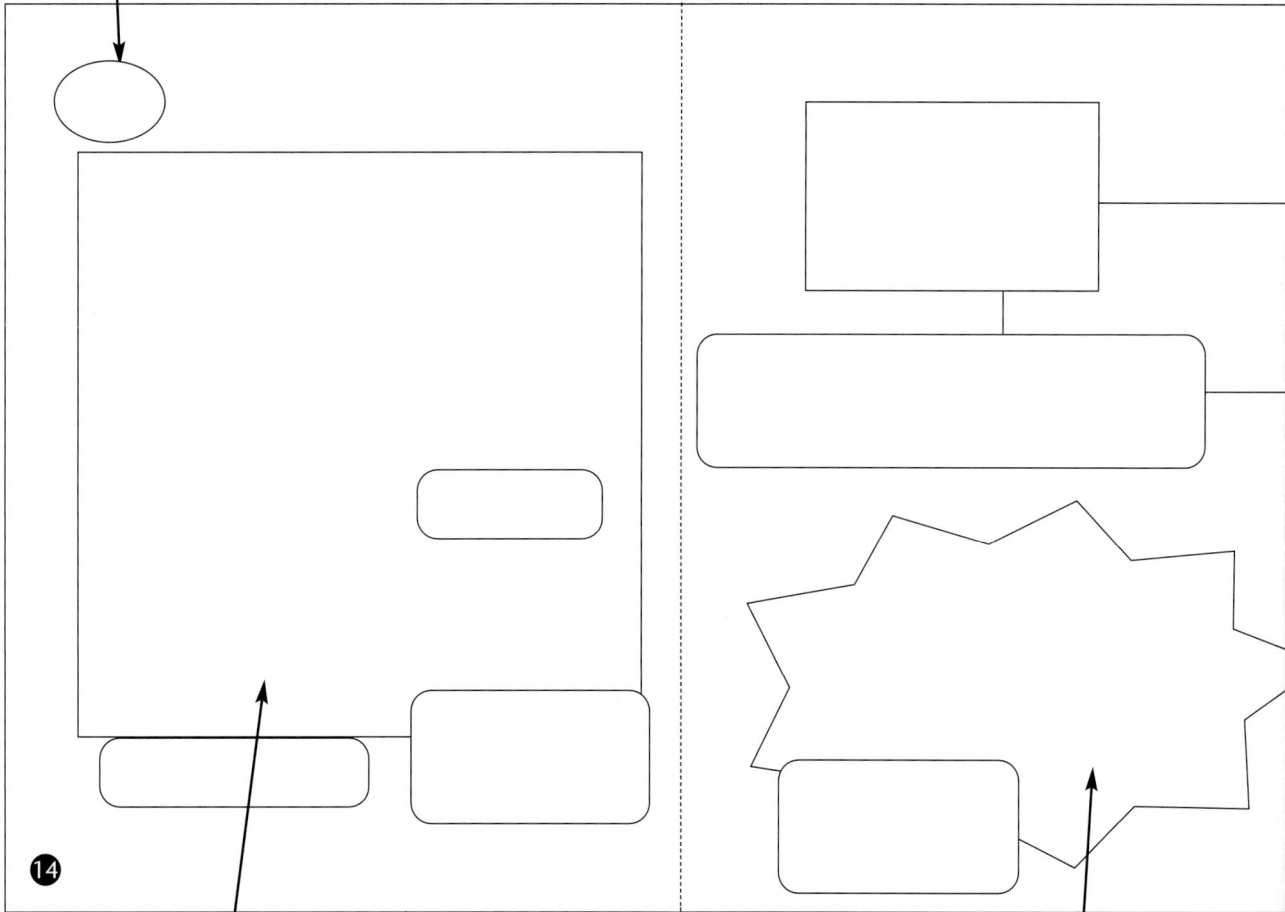

23 Main text

★ *How does the game start?*
★ *Which part of the alien must you draw first?*

24 Illustrations and main text

★ *What do these illustrations show?* Make sure the children understand the conventions and can match information from the text with each of the pictures.
★ *How do you win this game?*

14

25 Look back

This is not main text, so children may need some help with reading the questions.

16

Words and sentences

★ Can the children find the instructional verbs each time?
Show them that sometimes an instruction begins with an expression of time followed by a comma. Now can they find the verbs?

Making meaning

★ *Do you think the alien must look like the one in the book?*
Talk about features the alien must have, e.g. two eyes, four legs, one of each other features; but emphasise that the colour, positioning of the eyes/legs are the decision of each player.

Guided reading stages

Follow the three stages. Pace your session according to the focus you are following (e.g. content, literacy objective) and children's interests. Stage 2 may take more sessions than the other stages.

1 Introduce the book

★ *What do you think this book is going to be about?* Discuss title, blurb and cover images.

★ *What games do you play at wet playtime? What kind of text type do you think the book will be?* Explain to the children that thinking about this will help them understand the book better. List the words they know and guide them to the 'content and tricky' words listed on the front if possible.

★ *What do you think you can find out from this book?* Look at the contents page and browse through the book. Make a note of the children's ideas and encourage them to ask questions.

★ *How does this book work?* Talk about the overall 'shape' of the book. Point out that there are three games. The first and third are straight-forward instructions texts; the second is presented as a cartoon strip.

★ *Look at the way each page is set out.* Point out: Headings; Main text identification (black text on a yellow background).

2 Read the book

★ As the children read, use questions and guidance on the spread-by-spread notes in this booklet, pages 2–15, and the questions children asked in the introductory session. Children can read either just main text, or they can attempt some of the more challenging secondary text.

★ Encourage the children to spend time considering the pictures – they can learn a lot from 'reading the pictures'.

★ At the end of the session, talk about what the children have found in response to the questions you asked.

3 Revisit the book

★ *Have your questions been answered?* Remind children of the questions they asked in the first session. Discuss which have been answered and ask the children why they think some of the questions may not have been answered.

★ *If another group were to read this book, which questions should they be asked to think about?* Encourage the children to re-read parts of the book independently to think about appropriate questions.

★ *How did you read the 'tricky words'?* Focus on tricky words and discuss children's strategies for decoding them.

Follow on

Use these for '5 minute' session beginnings or endings, or to focus children's attention on word, sentence or text-level issues.

'**Tricky words**' suggests strategies for decoding words identified in the main text as being potentially challenging.

'**Words and sentences**' focuses on issues to do with vocabulary choice, punctuation, grammar and text layout.

'**Making meaning**' draws attention to bigger questions that arise from the text or pictures and help to develop comprehension.

OXFORD
UNIVERSITY PRESS

© Oxford University Press
First published 2004

www.OxfordPrimary.com

Sand, Kippers or Aliens?

Sarah Fleming

Contents

OXFORD
UNIVERSITY PRESS

What do you do at wet play?

Draw?

Read?

2

Play a board game?

Here are three games to play...

Game 1 The sand pudding

A game for 2 to 6 players.

You will need:

Try to cut away the sand but don't let the coin fall.

damp sand
a tray

a spade

a pencil
paper

a bowl

a coin

First, fill the bowl with sand.

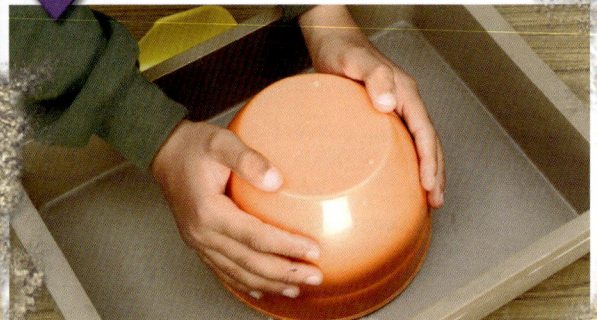

Then, turn the bowl upside down.

Next, take the bowl away.

Finally, put a coin on top of the sand pudding.

To play the game

Jo |
Dan
Josh
Zoe

1. In turn, use the spade to cut off a bit of the sand pudding.

2. If you make the coin fall, you get a point.

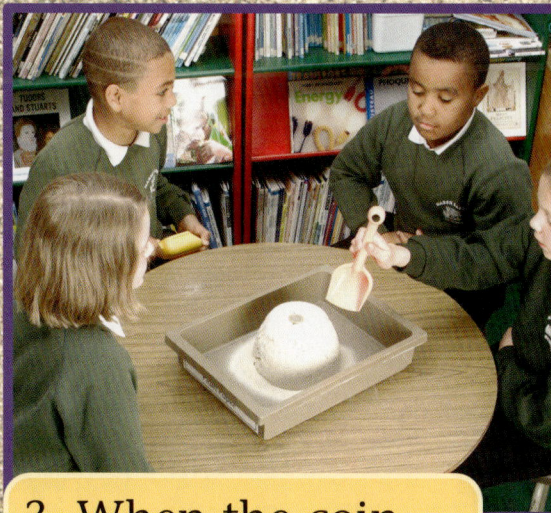

3. When the coin falls, make another pudding. Play again.

Jo |
Dan ||
Josh ||||
Zoe |||

4. The winner is the player with fewest points at the end of the game.

Later...
Ooops!
Look at my kipper!
My kipper is a shark!
My kipper's fat.

Now we need a place to race.
This can be the start.
This can be the finish.
On the carpet?

The alien race

A game for 2 to 6 players.

You will need:

a dice

a pencil
paper
(for each player)

Aim

To be the first to draw a whole alien.

How to play

When you throw these numbers on the dice, you can draw:

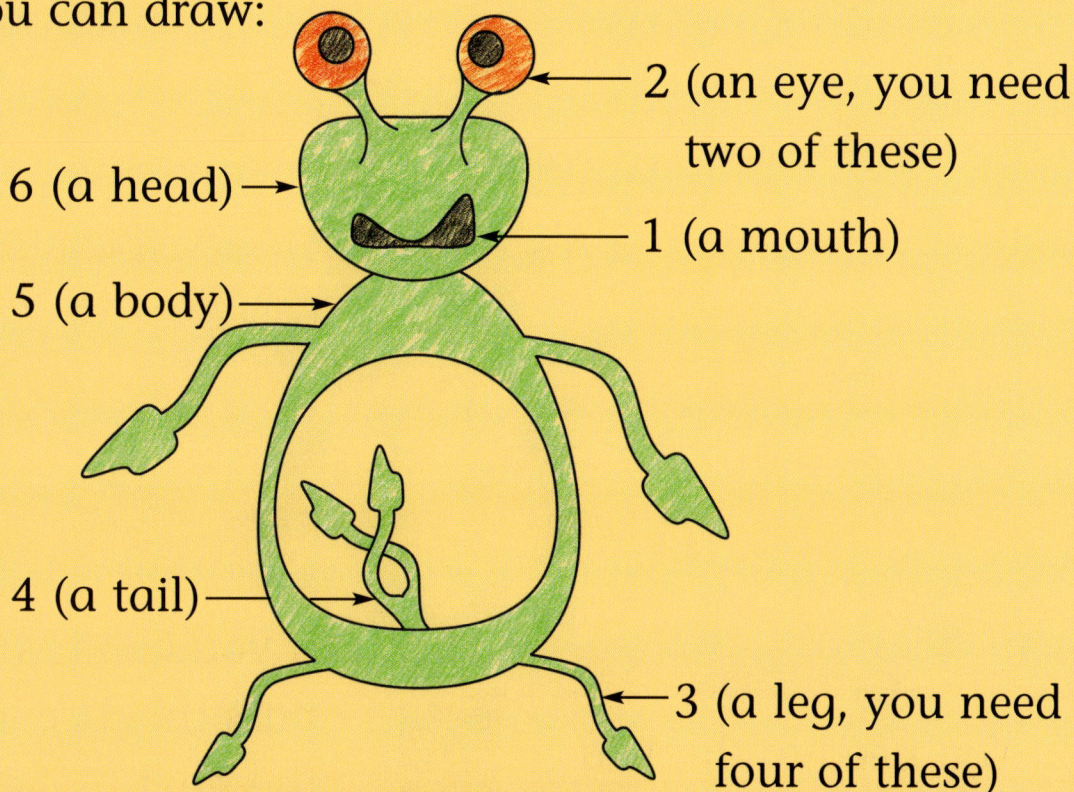

6 (a head) →

5 (a body) →

4 (a tail)

2 (an eye, you need two of these)

1 (a mouth)

3 (a leg, you need four of these)

13

1. Take turns to throw the dice.

2. You need to throw a six to start your alien.

3. If you can't go, pass the dice to the next player.

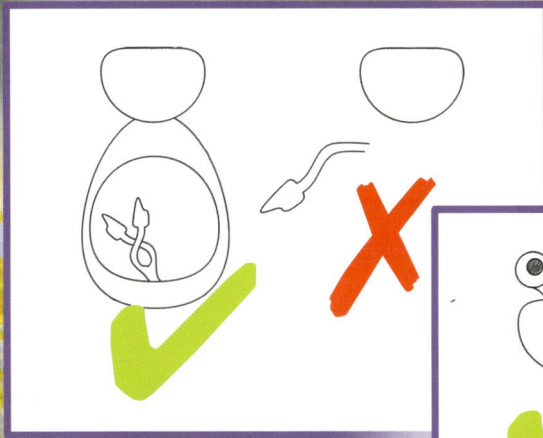

4. When you throw a number that you need, draw a bit of your alien. You need a body before the legs and tail. You need a head before the eyes and mouth.

5. The winner is the first to finish their alien.

Look back

1 Do you use wet or dry sand to make a sand pudding?
2 How many people joined in the kipper race?
3 In the alien race, what do you need to throw to draw a leg?
4 Which game do you think looks most fun? Why?

527188